Out of this Word

THE CHESHIRE PRIZE FOR LITERATURE ANTHOLOGIES

Prize Flights: Stories from the Cheshire Prize for Literature 2003; edited by Ashley Chantler

Life Lines: Poems from the Cheshire Prize for Literature 2004; edited by Ashley Chantler

Word Weaving: Stories and Poems for Children from the Cheshire Prize for Literature 2005; edited by Jaki Brien

Edge Words: Stories from the Cheshire Prize for Literature 2006; edited by Peter Blair

Elements: Poems from the Cheshire Prize for Literature 2007; edited by Peter Blair

Wordscapes: Stories and Poems for Children from the Cheshire Prize for Literature 2008; edited by Jaki Brien

Zoo: Short Stories from the Cheshire Prize for Literature 2009; edited by Emma Rees

Still Life: Poetry from the Cheshire Prize for Literature 2010; edited by Emma Rees

Wordlife: Poems and Stories for Children from the Cheshire Prize for Literature 2011; edited by Jaki Brien

Lost and Found: Short Stories from the Cheshire Prize for Literature 2012; edited by Emma Rees

Great Escapes: Poetry from the Cheshire Prize for Literature 2013; edited by Emma Rees

Out of this Word

Stories and Poems for Children from the Cheshire Prize for Literature 2014

Edited by Jaki Brien

University of Chester Press

First published 2015
by University of Chester Press
Parkgate Road
Chester CH1 4BJ

Printed and bound in the UK by the
LIS Print Unit
University of Chester
Cover designed by the LIS Graphics Team
University of Chester

Editorial Material
© University of Chester, 2015
Foreword, Stories and Poems
© the respective authors, 2015
Front cover image
© Brian Cosgrove

All Rights Reserved
No part of this publication may be reproduced, stored in a retrieval system or transmitted in any form or by any means without the prior permission of the copyright owner, other than as permitted by UK copyright legislation or under the terms and conditions of a recognised copyright licensing scheme

A catalogue record of this book is available
from the British Library

ISBN 978-1-908258-25-0

In memory of

Professor Henry Pearson

CONTENTS

Contributors	ix
Foreword	xiii
Badger *Tanya D. Ravenswater*	1
Turbo Wheels and the Bomb Squad *Catherine Bruton*	3
Champion Snail Face *Barbara Corfield*	8
Owt for Nowt *Liz Hedgecock*	11
Volcanoes are Rude!! *Linda Houlton*	14
The Boy Who Flew *Eric Twist*	16
The Enchanted Cat *Annette Albuquerque*	22
Scary Night *Eve Armstrong*	28
Who Goes There? *Thomas J. Arnold*	30

Out of this Word

Cannibal Gran *Pauline Barnett*	36
Second Chances *Lucy Carman*	38
The Story of a King Who Played Statues with a Little Girl *Joyce Fox*	44
Harriet *Laura Harrhy*	49
Don't Tell Sarah *Susan Hoffmann*	55
The Apprentice House *Jonathan Mayman*	61
Songs from the Animal Kingdom *Gill McEvoy*	62
Witch Way *Irene Moor*	66
Cat by the Garden Pool *Don Nixon*	68
Flypie and Doodlebug *Lynn Shelley*	69
Upadownalong *Martin Staton*	75

CONTRIBUTORS

Annette Albuquerque grew up in Chester, studied in Manchester and spent several years happily messing about in London before coming home. Currently, Annette is owned by a handsome marmalade cat who graciously shares her attentions with her husband and son.

Eve Armstrong is a retired primary school Head Teacher. She has a son and daughter and three grandchildren. Her hobbies include poetry writing and watercolour painting. She has been a WI member for over thirty years.

Thomas J. Arnold (Tom) lives in Chester and runs his own I.T. and engineering business. He has three young children and a lovely Irish wife who keep him in check. He has written a few books. Eventually, he plans on getting them all published and turned into movies.

Pauline Barnett, closet writer since her teens, divides her time between nurturing her chickens and writing verse, short stories and children's books. Not one for procrastination or impulsive leaps, she has also commenced her first adult novel, a mere thirty-five years in gestation.

Catherine Bruton was born in Warrington and spent her childhood in Lymm. The author of critically acclaimed novels for young people including *We Can be Heroes*, *Pop!* (set at Fiddler's Ferry) and *I Predict a Riot*, she was described by *The Guardian* as, 'one of the finest teen writers of recent years'.

Out of this Word

Lucy Carman is a freelance writer and home-based carer working with the elderly. She lives in Poynton, Cheshire with her husband and three children. Her great ambition is to write a children's novel.

Barbara Corfield graduated with a First-Class (Hons) degree this year but claims it pales into insignificance to receiving an award from the Cheshire Prize. Her enthusiastic children and encouraging husband support her inclusion of disability within her children's stories. Beware, she draws inspiration from everyone she meets!

Joyce Fox took her first Creative Writing course twenty-one years ago when she retired. She has been attending courses ever since – in Florida where she spends the winters, and at home in Manchester where she runs her own small group.

Laura Harrhy's writing reflects the world inside her head. Her imagination spills over into real life; everything and everyone has a story to tell, and most people take most things too seriously (particularly bosses and employment). One of her stories was included in the 2012 Cheshire Prize Anthology. She currently lives in beautiful Chester.

Liz Hedgecock grew up in South London, did an English degree, and then took forever to start writing. She now lives in Cheshire, and fits in as much writing as she can in the spaces between work, raising a family, and picking up Lego.

Contributors

Susan Hoffmann (Sue) has had sixteen short stories published in anthologies, newspapers, magazines and online and has won three writing competitions. In May 2013 her fantasy novel *High King* was published by Circaidy Gregory Press.

Linda Houlton lives and works in Malpas. Her poem 'Twelve Men and a Cheeseboard' was included in a previous Cheshire Prize Anthology. She is currently working on an anthology entitled *Of all the Gin Joints* which involves poetry about pubs, wine bars and alcohol. She admits to enjoying the research.

Jonathan Mayman lives in Chester. Married with two sons and two grandchildren, he is a solicitor by profession. His enthusiasms include sport, travel, history and all of the Arts – particularly music and poetry which he considers to be closely allied.

Gill McEvoy runs several regular poetry groups in Chester. She has published five collections: *Uncertain Days*, *A Sampler* and *The First Telling* (Happenstance Press, 2006, 2008, 2014); *The Plucking Shed* and *Rise* (Cinnamon Press, 2010, 2013). She is one of six featured poets in *Caboodle* (forthcoming from Prole books). Gill is a Hawthornden Fellow.

Irene Moor was born in Altrincham, grew up in Manchester and did a nursery nursing course at Newton-le-Willows. She has written poems since her early school days 'Just for Fun!' but always with childhood in mind. She lives with her husband; they have two daughters and two grandsons.

Don Nixon was a very successful writer of novels, poetry and short stories. His work is represented in several Cheshire Prize collections as well as magazines and anthologies in the UK, North America and Italy. He also won poetry competitions in Ireland and Italy. A true friend of the Cheshire Prize for Literature, Don died in the autumn of 2014.

Tanya D. Ravenswater was born in Northern Ireland but has been living in Cheshire for over twenty years. Writing poetry and fiction for all ages, Tanya is particularly inspired by the natural world; also by the diversity of human experience. There are so many worlds within worlds, stories within stories.

Lynn Shelley started telling stories when she was eight and has never stopped. An ex-primary school teacher, this is the first short story she has written for children but she has written several full-length children's books which she hopes to see published.

Martin Staton retired two years ago from a career in I.T. Married with two children and two granddaughters he now spends more time following his passion for writing. He has completed three novels, one of which is available as an e-book, and many short stories and poems.

Eric Twist has written poems and short stories – some of which have appeared in the anthology: *Thinking in Ink*. Plays and sketches (comedy) are his other passion. He says he would write if no-one ever read his work – but it's nice when they do!

FOREWORD

Out of this Word? I hope the title of the anthology from the 2014 High Sheriff's Cheshire Prize for Literature competition is much more than a foolish pun. Words have such power to take us out of our world and to create new, mysterious and extraordinary worlds of imagination. In the hands of a skilful writer, words create worlds. When writing for young readers, the magical power of words is always at the front of our minds. We make the shapes and broad strokes of the magic which every reader interprets as she chooses. Out of the writer's words, the reader's own imaginary world grows, unique and splendid. This is the strange symbiosis which turns children who can read into children who love to read. In turn, these young readers, inspired and taught by great writing, explore their own imagination through writing. And so the next generation of writers is created, nourished by their reading so they, in turn, can inspire another generation. So much comes out of the words we offer the young.

It is always inspiring to read the entries for the High Sheriff's Cheshire Prize for Literature. When the pile of scripts arrives, judges are delighted by the wonderful range of enthusiasts for the written word who are prepared to do that most vulnerable of things: put their words forward for a competition. More than ever before, the writers this year showed a depth of understanding about what inspires, intrigues and delights young children. The brave and talented people whose work is represented in this book certainly are great advocates for what is best in literature written for young readers.

Out of this Word

It would be wonderful to have the space to explain exactly why each piece in this anthology caught the judges' eyes and hearts. Sadly, I haven't this luxury so will, instead, focus on Don Dixon whose splendid poem *Cat by the Garden Pool* is on page 68. Don had a wonderful eye for the unusual, an ability to make us see simple things in new ways and an inventive delight in both the everyday and the extraordinary. What is more, he had skill with words to communicate his ideas with vivid grace. He entered the competition every year and was almost never out of the 'top twenty'. With his enthusiasm, talent and originality, Don epitomised everything which the Cheshire Prize stands for. We will miss him greatly.

It is the happy task of an editor to bring on to the glare of the page those very people who would so much rather stay in the shadows. The sponsorship of MBNA has enabled the competition to grow into the prestigious award it has become. At the University of Chester, the work of the Corporate Communications team, University of Chester Press, Graphics team and Print Unit steers the competition through from the first advert to the production of this anthology with remarkably good-natured proficiency. The utterly gorgeous cover illustration is by Dr Brian Cosgrove who has conveyed everything we hope our words will achieve for young readers. Brian was a splendid guest of honour at the Awards Evening in the autumn, bringing an enthusiasm and precision to consideration of the written word which characterised his BAFTA award winning version of *The Wind in the Willows* and his many series for children (and discerning adults) such as *Count Duckula* and *Dangermouse*. His honorary Doctorate of Letters from the University Chester in November 2014 was awarded in recognition of

Foreword

his outstanding contribution to the Arts. I am still slightly dazed that he agreed to create this picture for the anthology and am, needless to say, very grateful. When working with people like these, the work of an editor is a complete doddle. I am fortunate indeed and thank them all.

So, here's to the Cheshire Prize! Long may it flourish.

Jaki Brien

BADGER

Tanya D. Ravenswater

Lifting turf
his silver-grassed back
contours earth.

Shy? More *wry*.
Wary. Bemused by us.
Suspicious of those
who might impose
their idea of society.

He Grey,
underworldly,
transformer of clay.

He Brock,
harlequin white-black,
scavenger warlock.

He of The Quiet,
bulb, worm driven
inward, labyrinthine.

He of the frank bark,
growl, snort and chitter,
yelp, churr and kecker.

Out of this Word

He of scat iridescent,
carapace alchemist,
balancing dark-light.

He of The Subtle Mind,
of original spacious
ground, unfathomable.

Unsociable?
More discerning.
Comfortable with kin.
Fiercely protective
of Sett and Clan.

Root neighbour,
in soil, in soul deep,
He Badger.

TURBO WHEELS AND THE BOMB SQUAD

Catherine Bruton

There used to be a roller rink in our town. Sandwiched between the railway station and the soap-flake factory, the Rink was the centre of our world. When I was twelve years old, time was measured in days, hours, and minutes till Rink night; boys were rated on a scale from Darren the DJ (who my friend Lynne had once snogged) to Sick Skater boy. Everything I wore – right down to my electric blue eyeshadow – was chosen to match my Bauer Turbos.

Did I mention the Bauer Turbos? The Ferrari of wheeled footwear – sleek, black, with neon wheels and laces that glowed under the dazzling lights of the Rink glitter ball; anyone who was anyone wore Bauers. And nobody – except Nobodies – wore the vomit-coloured hire boots (with one exception – more of which later).

And *we* were Somebodies at the Rink – Claire#1, and Claire#2 and Lynne and Kit and Karen and I. With our shaggy perms and high-waisted jeans and our Bauer Turbos, we could skate backwards and do spins. But most important of all, our gang had a 'spot'. We were the Queens of the bottom left corner of the roller rink – by the girls' toilets and the chip bar. A gang of 'townie' girls hung out in the corner by the entrance; Darren the DJ's pulpit was in the top left corner and the Skater Boys' domain was the top right, by the skate ramp.

But we ruled the bottom left corner. On Rink nights we perched on the edge, swinging our Bauers, checking out the Skater Boys and watching the Nobodies stumble by in their sick-coloured hire boots.

'Cos only Nobodies wore sick boots.

Did I mention the one exception to that rule? The one Somebody who still suffered the indignity of wearing sick boots? That was me.

OK, so I may have given the impression that I owned a pair of Bauer Turbos but in fact I didn't. And the fact that I didn't was possibly the greatest tragedy of my teenage life.

"You want them; you save up for them," my dad said. My mum agreed with him – as usual. I cried and begged and pleaded – told them they were ruining my life – but they didn't give in.

Bauer Turbos cost £70 – which was a lot of money in 1986, when you only got 50p a week pocket money. It had taken me fifteen months to save up. Fifteen months of wearing sick boots, fifteen months of being ignored by Tim#2 – sexiest Skater Boy at the Rink – who I knew would never look my way till I changed my wheels. But now, finally, I had seven crumpled £10 notes burning a hole in my pocket and I was catching the bus to town with Claire#1 to buy my Bauers.

Only we missed the bus. Actually, it probably saved my life but I didn't realise that at the time, or I probably wouldn't have got so mad at my kid brother for dropping Dad's house keys in the fish bowl – which is what made us late 'cos no one was allowed to go out till he found them. I felt bad about that later. Actually, if I'd known just how things were going to turn out, I'd have been way nicer to my brother generally. But I didn't. So I wasn't.

Anyway, we caught the next bus and me and Claire#1 spent the journey talking about Tim#2 (there must have been a Tim#1 once but nobody remembered him) and

Turbo Wheels and the Bomb Squad

Padgate Paz (who Claire#1 fancied) and then we got off the bus and that was when the bomb went off.

Did I mention there was a bomb in this story? It was a surprise to us too. 'Cos you're never expecting a bomb are you? Not on a Saturday afternoon – in a quiet northern town where nothing happens, and which few people had even heard of.

And if you're not expecting a bomb you don't even realise it is one at first. I just remember there was just this weird tightening in the air, a sound like everything crumpling and then stuff flying – bricks and dust. And then – after a long, long second – people shouting and screaming. And my friend Claire was clutching her head and yelling about her rat's tail. She had one of those rat's tails in her hair – like Adam Ant or Bananarama – and for some reason she was convinced it had been blown off by the blast. I remember thinking it was a weird thing to be going on about. But then, all I could think about was my Bauer Turbos. And how I needed to get them. And I wasn't going to let a silly thing like the town being blown up stop me.

Claire#1 was crying too much to know what to do, so I dragged her away from the blast, toward the Rink, but it was cut off. And suddenly there were police everywhere – closing off roads, herding us into a park in the centre of town.

So that was where we ended up – us and about 500 other people who'd been minding their own business shopping on a sunny Saturday when a bomb had gone off. Everyone was talking about the IRA – and about casualties – and the police searching for more bombs. And Claire#1 was having a panic attack because she was SURE we were both going to be killed. But all I could think about was not being able to get my Bauers.

It turned out – afterwards of course – that there had been a bomb right there. Right there in the park. It was faulty so it hadn't gone off – which was a good job really, or else 500 people would have gone sky high and then the police would have looked pretty silly.

They let us all go in the end. And I got my Bauers. With electric blue and neon pink laces and matching wheels. And they were utterly and completely beautiful.

I'd worried the Rink wouldn't open that night – because of the bomb and the people who had been hurt – but our roller rink, 'Would not let itself be defeated by terrorism'. And so I wore my Bauers and I skated backwards under the rotating jewels of the glitter ball and I smiled at Tim#2 and he smiled back – he definitely smiled back – and Claire#1 snogged Padgate Paz behind the DJ booth. And it should have been perfect.

And then, at one point Darren the DJ announced that two boys had been killed in the bomb blast. He turned off the decks and held a minute's silence. The glitter ball stopped spinning and the skater boys stopped turning loops and it was so weirdly silent in the roller rink that for the first time I noticed how shabby it was. How it was only really a tatty warehouse with peeling paint and a smell of stale chips hanging in the air. And in the weird half-light I looked down at my Bauers and even they didn't seem so stellar as they had before. They looked too big, too bright, too brash.

It wasn't my brother, by the way. You were thinking my brother was one of those boys who was killed, weren't you? But it wasn't him. It was one of his friends. A kid from school with a bright smile who he played football with. He was also called Tim – just like my rink heart-throb (who, incidentally, broke his leg a couple of weeks later and gave up skating for good so I never did get to snog him in the end).

And the other boy who was killed – the little boy with a face like an angel who was on the front page of every newspaper – I didn't know him at all. I suppose I didn't really know Tim either. But still – maybe it was delayed shock or something – because when it was all over, and the glamour of the new boots and being nearly killed had faded, I couldn't stop thinking about those two boys.

And when, six months later, they closed the Rink and our world imploded – well, mine didn't really. I mean, I cried the night they closed it down – it was on my thirteenth birthday – but only because all the Bauer gang did. But I think for me something had already shifted.

Maybe it was my boots – my Formula One footwear – I'd thought they'd make me feel like Somebody, make me shimmer like a glitter ball, inside and out. But it was funny – all upside down, topsy-turvy really – because when the bomb went off all I could think about was my Turbo boots. And then afterwards, when it was over, I looked at my boots and all could think of was the boys and the bomb.

And that probably goes to show something – as my mum would say. Although I'm still not sure I know exactly what.

CHAMPION SNAIL FACE

Barbara Corfield

Tomorrow, I would like to break a world record for the most snails stuck to my face. I looked it up in the *Guinness World Records* book. The record currently stands at seven, but I reckon I could beat that. I think I could fit about four or five on my forehead. Then one on my nose, although I'm not sure if I could balance it, so I will have to lie down. If I lie down, could I swallow one by accident? I don't know if a snail can survive passing through the digestive system, so I can't risk one going down my throat. Maybe if it curled up inside its shell really tight, and used its goo to build a thick layer at the entrance, maybe the acid in my stomach wouldn't kill it? Anyway, I could definitely get a snail or two on my chin, three on each cheek, and one on each eyelid. As it is summer time but pouring with rain, there are lots of snails in my garden to choose from, all hiding in the flower bed, picking holes in Mum's marigold leaves. I will pick small snails and smash that record (but not the snails).

When I was about three or four, I used to lick snails, Mum said. Then I used to lick the floor. I wanted to be a snail, so would slobber puddles of spit along the path to try and make my own trail. I don't lick them now, but would love to have a shell on my back. Then when my teacher asks me to do maths, I could pull the shell over my head and disappear. I would sit inside my shell, plug in my headphones and listen to my music until home time. My parents would be called by the Head Teacher to explain my actions, but they would be snails too. They'd create a slithery path right up to the Head's office door, so when she came out to greet them, she would go flying on the slimy floor, land on her bottom and have to cancel the meeting.

The only problem with snails is that the shell is their only protection. They have no scorpion-like sting, or spikes. I'm like the class snail in room 12B, full of giant male birds. Today, a black hawk called Connor flew at me. He pecked my shell so hard that he broke a hole in it. My teacher says that the hole can be mended, but I don't think it will be the same again, stuck together with papier-mâché promises and sticky tape apologies. The teacher asked me to write my feelings down on a piece of paper and put it into the feelings box because I couldn't stop crying. My Mum says it's because I am kind and sensitive, so don't understand the behaviour of mean boys. My teacher says it's because I need to 'grow a thick skin'. If that means I have to be a blackbird or an eagle and peck at small creatures, then I'm happier being a snail with a glued up shell.

I'm sorry. I didn't introduce myself. How rude of me. I am James, I am nine years old and I live at number 13 Ottersley Avenue. I have brown hair and green eyes. I like to eat lasagne and I have Down's syndrome. My Mum says that by putting that at the end of the sentence, people will have already got to know me. If I were not writing to you, but talking to you, you would know I had Down's syndrome. That's because you can see it in my face. If you can't see properly, you have glasses and I can see them on your face. If you have freckles on your face then I know you will probably burn in the sun. I don't have freckles, but I would like them. If you saw my face, then you would know I am a nice person because I smile a lot. If I could meet you, I would shake you by the hand. If you are a lady, I would kiss you on the cheek. That's because I am a gentleman.

So, tomorrow I will break a world record. I will fit lots of snails on my face, and my Mum is going to take a photograph of me to send to the *Guinness World Records*. I think they are in London. You should buy the world records book next year and look for me. I might be under the section on children, or disabled people or on a page about snails.

James ☺☺☺

OWT FOR NOWT

Liz Hedgecock

"I'm sorry, Jazz." Mum put the iron down. "We can't afford it. There's always your cousin Courtney's bike ..."

Another hand-me-down. I made a sourpuss face. I couldn't help it. Courtney's bike, which she'd outgrown, was like new. Sugar pink, with streamers on the handlebars and a princess on the chain guard. I wouldn't be caught dead on it. Especially not at high school. I loved my old bike but my knees were under my chin. I just needed a red nose and a clown wig.

I thought fast. "Mum, it's an investment. At high school I'd have to pay for the bus every day. The bike would save lots of money ..."

Mum came to sit at the breakfast bar with me. "Do you remember Great-Granny Nora?"

I thought of a bristly chin, wool and humbugs. "Sort of."

"Well, she used to say 'You can't get owt for nowt.'" Mum smiled. "That means you can't get something for nothing. Jazz, you're a big girl now, so I'll be honest. Is that OK?"

Something made me swallow, hard.

"Every month I get paid, and I take out the money for rent, and gas and electricity, and water, and food, and the bus to work. And I used to have a little left over to save, or spend on something nice."

She swallowed hard, too. "But since the rent went up, I take those bills away from what comes in, and there's

Out of this Word

nothing left. So a new bike, at £150, isn't possible. Not for nothing." Her voice was kind. "Do you see?"

"Yes."

How could I make something out of nothing?

***

I went to see my future bike on Saturday. My silver racer, my thoroughbred, my freedom. Mr Jones said if I could find the money, he'd sell me the bike for £125.

It was almost as impossible as before.

I knocked on for Amber, and we went to our secret place. It's only the end bit of the walkway outside our flats, but we could talk in private.

"Could you make something and sell it?"

"It's a start." We went to my room and looked at the unopened birthday craft kits. Amber likes that sort of thing, so she helped me string beads and paint picture frames and make pompom animals.

Mum said she was pleased I was keeping myself busy.

On Monday we took it all to the school bits and bobs shop. Mrs Watson looked over her glasses at me, wrote it down in a little black book, and said to come back next week. And there was nothing to do but wait.

But the next Saturday I went to see my bike and Mr Jones said "Do you have the money yet?"

I said no.

"Ah." He started rearranging the energy bars.

"Why?"

After a lot of tidying, he told me all the prices were going up. In two weeks, my bike would cost £180.

***

Owt for Nowt

I went along to the shop at lunch on Monday. Mrs Watson reached for the black book, and lifted the red cash box from under the table. "You made £10."

"Thank you." I looked at the money in my palm.

"Were you expecting more?"

"No, it's not that. I – I don't know what to do. Just - one thing of my very own ..."

And the whole story came out. The bike, and Mum, and Courtney's horrible princess bike, and the two weeks.

"Mm." said Mrs Watson. "So you need to make money quickly, without much to start with."

"Yes!" I was one big grin.

VOLCANOES ARE RUDE!!

Linda Houlton

VOLCANOES ARE RUDE!!!
I love volcanoes
I love them to bits
I think they're flametastic
With their smouldering pits.
But after much thought
I've been forced to conclude
I love volcanoes
Because they are RUDE!!

First they BELCH smoke
Then they throw rocks
They make you fall over
With huge aftershocks
They ERUPT, they EXPLODE
When they're in a bad mood
I love volcanoes
Because they are RUDE!!

Then they SPIT pebbles
Then they HURL lava
There's a bad tempered volcano
GRUMBLES just west of Java
Causes trouble with rubble
It's incredibly CRUDE
I love volcanoes
Because they are RUDE!!

Volcanoes are Rude!!

I love volcanoes
They're magmastically cool
They're always in trouble
In Bad Mountain school
Their teachers all shout
'You have poor attitude!'
I love volcanoes
Because they are RUDE!!

I love volcanoes
At the Hazard World Cup
They HARASS the hurricanes
Trip the tornadoes up
The referees hate them
And choose to exclude
The volatile volcanoes
Because they are RUDE!!

I love volcanoes
I love them to bits
I think they're flametastic
With their smouldering pits.
But after much thought
I've been forced to conclude
I love volcanoes
Because they are REALLY REALLY REALLY RUDE!!

THE BOY WHO FLEW

Eric Twist

Thomas had always wanted to fly. That's probably not unusual for an eight-year-old boy but Thomas was really serious about it. He lived on a farm and he would spend his weekends out in the fields, running up and down with his arms outstretched, like an aeroplane.

And then, one day, he took off.

He felt a bit nervous, stretched out full length, his arms flapping like a bird's wings. So he didn't go very high at first, just about three or four feet off the ground. But he easily cleared the hedge at the end of the field and found that he could glide and turn by altering the angle of his arm 'wings'. It was breath-taking. The most fantastic feeling he had ever had. He was flying.

He just had to show his parents. So he turned and flew back up to the farm and landed in the farmyard.

    He burst into the kitchen. "I can fly," he blurted out. "Come and see."

    "Yes, of course, love – when you've eaten your tea," his mother smiled.

    "But …"

    "Do as you mother says," said his father, pausing his forkful of sausage halfway to his mouth. He knew there was no point in arguing, so Thomas sat down and tried to eat his sausage, mash and green beans. He hated green beans.

"And don't go throwing it down," cautioned his mother. "You'll give yourself indigestion."

When finally, the meal was over, Thomas pushed back his chair "Come on. Please. Now." His father gave a sigh, exchanged a look with his wife, and they both followed Thomas outside into the yard.

"Now you just stand there, and give me some room to take off."

He began his run. There was a low stone wall at the end of the yard and he felt he would have gained enough height to clear it easily. But he ran slap bang into it. Something was wrong. Bruised and shaken he walked back to have another try. His father was glancing at his watch. It was nearly milking time.

Thomas backed up further, to take a longer run. Again he failed to take off. Not even a couple of inches. But this time he managed to slow down just before he hit the wall. He was near tears. He just couldn't understand it.

"Perhaps you need some flying lessons," laughed his dad. "Come on, I'm going to milk the cows."

But Thomas couldn't face cows after this massive disappointment. Surely he hadn't imagined it all. He really had been flying, hadn't he? He looked around. The farmyard was empty. "I'll just have one more go." He said to himself.

He ran, full tilt, across the yard. The wall was coming up fast – and then suddenly it was dropping away beneath him. He was soaring gracefully up into the sky.

But how was it that he could fly now and yet couldn't fly when his parents were watching? Then it dawned on him.

Out of this Word

He could only fly when no one was looking at him. This took a bit of a shine off the whole thing. I mean what's the point of being able to fly if you can't show anyone?

Disappointed, he banked to the left in a big arc and began to glide back over the wall, and into the yard. But someone *was* watching him! Rufus, the farm's sheepdog, was staring up at him and barking excitedly. Tom was puzzled – how was it that he could fly if an animal was watching, but not when humans were?

He couldn't think of an answer. But then he had an idea. His dad was a keen photographer and had often shown Thomas his camera and tried to explain how it worked. Thomas hadn't been particularly interested but had tried to show some enthusiasm, just to please his dad. Now he was glad he had paid some attention.

The camera was kept in a cupboard, in the kitchen; it was always loaded with film, ready for that sudden 'photo-opportunity' his dad was always waiting for. What better photo-opportunity than this! "The camera never lies," his dad always said. Well, if Thomas took some photos *from the air* his parents would *have* to believe he could fly!

Tom's dad was likely to be some time – there were a lot of cows to be milked – and his mother had taken the car to go shopping in the village. Even so, he felt a bit nervous as he opened the cupboard door and took out the camera. He checked that it was loaded with film.

He hung the camera around his neck and secured it to his chest with a piece of string from the kitchen drawer. His dad had shown him how you could set it so it took a photo every five seconds, automatically. Making the necessary adjustments, Thomas went outside.

The yard was empty except for Rufus, asleep in a patch of sunshine. Thomas began his run, arms flapping. The stone wall approached at speed and then he was over it and soaring up into the blue sky. He banked and turned back over the yard. Rufus had woken up and was staring up at him. Dad had lots of photos of Rufus but none like this, Tom thought as he swooped low over the dog, camera clicking.

This was wonderful. Thomas continued taking pictures until, in the distance he saw a car approaching. *His mother's car.* She was on her way back.

Thomas had to get down before she arrived. What would happen if he were still in the air when she drove into the yard? Would he fall to the ground like a stone? He couldn't risk it. Turning, he glided down. Unfortunately he misjudged the angle of his descent and caught his toe on the top of the wall. Next minute he was lying in a dusty heap next to Rufus, who was now barking furiously.

Then his mother was kneeling anxiously beside him. "Oh, Thomas!" she wailed. Running footsteps. His father arrived and helped his son to his feet. "Are you alright? What were you doing?"

Apart from being shaken and bruised, Thomas seemed none the worse for his accident. But the same could not be said for the camera; there was a dent in the metal body and the lens was cracked. The camera back had sprung open exposing the film to light. Thomas hurriedly closed it and snapped the catch. But he knew it was too late; the film would be ruined.

His father had seen it too. "My camera!" he shouted.

Thomas tried to explain. When he had finished his father looked serious but he spoke gently. "It doesn't matter about the camera – it's about time I changed to digital, anyway – but you must stop all these lies. I don't want to hear another word about flying – ever."

It was the end of Thomas's flying – at least for some time.

***

Thomas grew up, and became 'Tom'. And, as soon as he was old enough, he joined the Royal Air Force and was accepted for pilot training. It was a great day for both Tom and his parents when he returned to the farm, his 'wings' proudly displayed over the left breast pocket of his dress uniform.

He had a week's leave before being posted to his new squadron and he spent it helping his dad on the farm. Rufus had died some years ago, and Tom missed him.

On Saturday evening his dad drove Tom to the station. It was late when Tom's dad got back to the farm. He went straight to his study. Sitting down at his desk, he unlocked the top left hand drawer and took out a photo wallet, the sort they give you when you collect your prints from the processors, and taking out the photos he spread them on the desk.

They were not very good photographs; there were white steaks across them where light had got into the camera, and most were blurred. But some were quite recognisable: the shot of a red tractor, looking almost like a toy in a model farmyard; another of the tops of two barns; one of the roof of a shippen; another of a patchwork of fields; and two or three of the blurred green treetops that looked as if they were rushing past the camera. But the photo that really stood out was of a dog. It was sitting in a patch of sunlight in the middle of a farmyard, looking up into the air, straight into the camera lens, with a puzzled but pleased look on its face. There was no mistaking Rufus.

Tom's dad looked at the photos for a long time – then he switched on the shredder.

THE ENCHANTED CAT

Annette Albuquerque

Dear Mrs Banks,

I expect you are wondering what has happened to Daisy. I shall explain.

This morning, we had a spelling test. I knew all the spellings because I learnt them all, after school, yesterday. I even missed *Bella the Brave* on television because I was determined to get them all right. And I did. I got twenty out of twenty, only nobody knows that because Daisy – yes, your daughter, Daisy Banks – collected all the test papers and she scribbled out my name at the top of my paper and wrote Daisy Banks; and she wrote my name on the top of her own paper. So Miss Judge gave me a big, fat zero while Daisy got a gold star. *My* gold star. My eyes narrowed. However, I like to think I am a forgiving sort of person so I decided to give Daisy a chance.

At playtime, I told Daisy that, if she confessed her crime, we would say no more about it. I am sorry to report that Daisy did not confess. Oh, no! Our next lesson was maths and we were working in groups on Shapes and Angles. Well, any idiot knows that a triangle with two equal sides is called isosceles. Any idiot except Daisy, that is. But she wanted to give the answer, so I told her. I like to be generous. "Isosceles," I said.

The Enchanted Cat

"I, sausages!" she shouted. Of course, the whole class fell about laughing and, of course, Daisy blamed me. Miss Judge blamed me, too.

"It's not very nice, is it, Angelica, to deliberately embarrass one of your friends like that?" she said; I hissed softly; and she kept me in at lunchtime.

I didn't mind staying in. I sharpened all the pencils and stacked the maths books and mixed the paints ready for art. It was peaceful; so, while I was doing all that, I had a good think. I thought about Daisy and her crimes against me and I concluded that it was not entirely Daisy's fault. I mean, it's not her fault that she has cabbage soup and stale bread for dinner every day because you can't afford proper food. It's not her fault that she has to sleep in a cupboard because you need her bedroom for the mysterious lodger who never goes out in daylight. It's not her fault that you have to leave her alone every night so you can go to Bingo to win some extra money, or that you always end up losing it instead. And it's certainly not her fault that Mr Banks is in prison for getting drunk and fighting in the street. No. Not her fault at all. And I know that problems at home can mean problems in school so I decided to forgive her. Again.

I gave Daisy all the best paintbrushes and the biggest sheet of paper and, when she came in from the playground, I went to sit next to her, even though – to be honest – she was extremely sweaty and smelt bad. But it can't be easy, having no running water at home.

I enjoy painting and I was particularly looking forward to today's lesson. We were painting 'My Favourite Character from Children's Literature' and I had chosen Roald Dahl's *Matilda*.

Daisy was doing Barbie. I pointed out, tactfully and because I wanted to help, that Barbie is a doll and doesn't count as a character from literature; but Daisy didn't want to be helped. She said, "Barbie's in a book, it's called *The Barbie Annual* and I've got it at home, so there!" And she poked out her tongue, which was very rude but then she has never been taught any better so what can you expect? (No offence.)

I was pleased with my Matilda: I had taken a lot of trouble over her. Daisy had taken a lot of trouble, too – or at least a lot of paint – but, let's be honest, she is no artist. Poor Barbie had a face like a potato, starfish hands and one leg twice the size of the other. She looked like the result of a terrible accident in the toy factory. Daisy caught me looking. She squinted at Matilda. "That's rubbish," she said; and, before I could stop her, she grabbed my wrist and plonked my hand into the pot of blue paint. She pulled it out and held it, dripping, over the table. Daisy is surprisingly strong for such an under-nourished and neglected child: possibly as a result of all that digging she is forced to do on your allotment. Anyway, for a dreadful moment, I thought she was going to mutilate Matilda with my own hand; but Daisy is cleverer than that. Splat! She smacked my hand down right in Barbie's face. Splat! Splat! Splat! Seconds later, Barbie had disappeared under multiple blue handprints, all mine, and Daisy was wailing and spurting real tears and pointing first at me and then at her ruined painting. Actually, 'ruined' is not quite the right word: I thought the handprints were a great improvement; but there was Miss Judge, glaring at me. You cannot reason with Miss Judge when she has that look on her face.

"Angelica Grace, are those your handprints?" she demanded.

The Enchanted Cat

"Yes," I said. What else could I say? My fingers flexed, splattering paint. Miss Judge had no alternative, she said. I was sent to Mr Cross: the Head.

It was while I was sitting outside Mr Cross's office that I began to wonder: why me? I mean: clearly, Daisy is very disturbed by her unfortunate home situation; but why me? Why doesn't she pick on Patrick or torment Tabitha or stitch up Stephanie? What have I done to bring down the full force of Daisy's deviousness upon my innocent head? Not only that, but why was Mr Cross keeping me waiting? Nobody was in there with him: I had put my ear to the door twice and there was no talking, unless it was in sign-language. Was he enjoying a five-course afternoon tea? Playing computer games? Perhaps he'd been tied up and gagged by intruders. It would serve him right. In fact, I knew why he was leaving me to sit there on a hard chair opposite the office so that Mrs Jones could keep giving me nasty looks: it was to make me nervous, to break me down and trick me into a false confession. Well, it wasn't going to work. I wasn't nervous: I was annoyed; I was bored; and I was missing the play rehearsal. I could hear the piano tinkling out the opening tune: The Enchanted Cat. It was my theme: I am The Enchanted Cat; or I was. The terrible truth flashed into my mind: Daisy wanted to be The Cat!

Sure enough, seconds later, there was Daisy, screeching out the words in her nasty, scratchy voice:

"I am The Cat, The Enchanted Cat,

I can cast a spell on you, just like that!"

Oh, really? We'll see about that, I thought. I sprang from my chair, blew a sarcastic kiss to Mrs Jones and stalked into the hall. Miss Judge tried to stop me. "Angelica Grace, what do you think you are doing?" But she hadn't a hope. I stood in front of Daisy Banks and threw my own spell straight into her sneaky face:

"*I* am The Cat, The Enchanted Cat!

You are nothing more than a scabby little rat!"

Then I turned around and went back to my chair outside Mr Cross's office.

It was pandemonium in the hall. Daisy was squeaking exactly like a frightened rat – she was already scabby, of course; and all the other children were shrieking and running about; and Miss Judge was yelling, "Be quiet! Sit down at once! Where is Daisy Banks? Eeeek! There's a rat!" It was very satisfying.

Despite all the noise and other teachers abandoning their classes to investigate, resulting in at least a hundred unsupervised children rampaging around the school, and Mrs Jones flapping around like a headless chicken in the safety of her office, Mr Cross has still not appeared. I think he might be dead. So I thought I should use the time to explain to you why your daughter has been turned into a rat. Don't worry: it's only a temporary spell; she should be herself again by tomorrow morning – I am tempted to add, 'unfortunately' but that would be uncharitable.

I suppose I should apologise. I know how hard things must be for you, what with your shoplifting conviction and the embarrassing medical condition that you don't like to talk

The Enchanted Cat

about. So, alright, I apologise. But Daisy had better watch out, in future. After all, I *am* The Enchanted Cat.

Yours sincerely,

Angelica Grace

SCARY NIGHT

Eve Armstrong

I woke up very suddenly, in the dead of night.
The curtains all were drawn; no chink of street-lamp light
Came in to help me work out what was lurking near my bed.
I held my breath and stayed so still, quite overcome with dread.

Then I pulled the duvet closer and shivered as I lay
Waiting for another sign and wished it could be day.
A BOOMING sound from in the hall chimed out the hour of three,
When all the world was fast asleep, except, of course, for me.

A tapping on the window added to my fear.
Was there someone out there, waiting to come here?
It could be just a tiny twig, blowing in the breeze
Or maybe something sinister, lurking in the trees!

But no, I had the feeling that this 'SOMETHING' was right here
Within this room, right by my bed, so very, very near.
Perhaps I was surrounded by creatures of the night,
Creeping close to pounce on me! I tried to reach the light.

Scary Night

My fingers couldn't find the switch. The lamp was out of reach.
My hands were shaking oh so much and I'd lost the power of speech.
I've never felt so frightened. Well, maybe that's not true,
I'd once been lost in London and not known what to do.

I could hear the sound of breathing, very close to me.
I kept my eyes shut tightly, afraid of what I'd see.
Could this house be haunted? You hear of such of strange things:
Of flying objects, ghostly sounds and a bell that sometimes rings.

I felt a hand upon my head and fingers in my hair!
Someone was sitting close to me, upon the bedside chair.
Then a sound, a tiny voice, whispered in my ear.
"Granny, can I sleep with you, while you're staying here?"

WHO GOES THERE?

Thomas J. Arnold

"There's someone behind us. Following."

"Where?" asked Ben. Voice quivering but trying to sound brave.

"There! There!" Ben's little sister Katy raised her arm straight ahead and pointed through the thick fog.

"It's just the field playing tricks on us," Ben told her.

"I knew we should have got the bus. We never should have walked home," said Katy.

Even Ben was regretting the decision. His words echoed back to him like a punch in the guts ... "I know a shortcut home from school. Through Cavalier's Field and across the river. Come on!" He'd urged his mates but none of them had the courage.

"You serious, Ben? You know what night it is?" That had been his best mate Danny.

"Yeah. So what?" But deep down he knew. Everyone in the village knew.

"Come on Sis," he said and reluctantly she followed suit. Trudging across the road; the sun slipping below the horizon as they tramped quietly home. The milky blot quickly smothered by a dense rolling fog that materialised within seconds of them taking the path across the field.

And now here they were, stuck in the middle of the potato field on the anniversary of the massacre. Ben could sense the prickling swirl of anticipation in the air. A sense of somebody there in the shadows. Watching. Stalking them. Deadly. Like a sniper eyeing his target down the barrel of his rifle sights. Up ahead Ben could hear the river tumbling and gurgling as it headed towards the Dee a few miles to the west in Chester.

"Nearly there ..." he said.

The heavy rush of the nearby river seemed to deaden Ben's senses. He'd walked this way a million times in the daylight. In the summer they often crossed the field and paddle in the river after school. But no-one crossed Cavalier's Field at night. Not even adults. Not even his dad.

He'd never forget that look on his dad's face "Ben. Once the sun sets, promise me you will never take that shortcut home. Do you understand? Never. Promise me! You or your sister take to that field ... and so help me God ..." The strange thing was the look on his face. It wasn't anger. Not anger. It was fear. Pure fear. And nothing of this world scared Ben's dad. He'd fought in Afghanistan, seen things that gave him nightmares. But this was something else. Something worse than the horrors of war.

Up ahead – the carcass of a great oak lay on its side. Its massive trunk and boughs bleached white with time. Its bark flailed bare to expose its ancient bones. Ben knew this tree. So did Katy. They picked up their pace.

"It's the stump! We're half way home!" yelped Katy as she ran ahead to place her hands on the old friend. It was cold like death against her fingers.

Ben clambered up onto the massive old trunk. It was smooth as glass and a thick layer of frost made balancing precarious at best. He raised his arms out like a high-wire act at the big-top and began to edge along the body of the dead tree. The drop was small – five maybe ten feet in certain places. But it gave Ben a feeling of security perched up high, out of reach of whatever lurked in the white haze that dogged them.

Katy sat for a second. Lost in her own thoughts.

She looked up, momentarily panicked, her older brother almost out of sight. She scanned the tree keenly until she saw his dark shadow balancing on the tree – arms outstretched in a pose that made Katy think of Jesus on the Cross. A crucifixion. It was a horrible thought and she quickly shook her head to rid it from her mind.

When she looked up, the shadow was approaching. Arms by its sides now. Which was better. "Come on Ben. I want to get moving. Let's go …"

No response.

"Ben?"

The figure approached. Walking sure-footed down the trunk towards her. "Stop playing games Ben …" trembling hysteria bubbling just below.

Still nothing. Just the dark figure coming at her through the white. "Stop it! Stop it now!"

Suddenly there was a jarring tug on her shoulder and her brother was reeling her round and dragging her off the stump. She screamed. The scream floating out into the great nothing of Cavalier's Field and falling like dandelion seeds into the ground. The scream sinking down into the soil with the soldier dead. She stared into her brother's hugely dilated pupils. Fizzing with adrenalin and wild panic.

"Quick! Move it, Sis!" he ordered her, like a sergeant-major yelling at his troops as they headed over the top.

She dropped her school bag and ran. She glanced over her shoulder to see the dark figure swooping towards them. It leapt off the log like a panther. Dark, sleek and menacing. And there was something in its hand. Large. Blade-like. A sword?

Who Goes There?

Ben and Katy ran hard. Their lives depending on it. Throats burning hot and filling with bile as they stumbled over the boggy potato field. Behind them came the figure.

"Don't look back. Just make it to the bridge. They can't cross running water ... they can't ..." Ben panted. Black spots flashing in front of his eyes. Exhaustion setting in as they hammered down the path. Mud spattering their faces, their uniform; feet mulchy and wet as they slammed them down through the puddles, leaving great muddy craters in the quagmire.

"There it is!" Ben shouted and urged Katy along. To the wooden footbridge up ahead. Behind them came an eerie caterwauling. Not an animal. But not quite human.

"Eerghhhhhhhhh!" again the eerie low-pitched guttural growl. Not far behind.

"Come on!" screamed Ben. His mouth was dry and his gums thick and pasty with exertion. Small lumps of dried spittle were beginning to freeze on his mouth and chin, covering him in a brittle sheen, like plaster of Paris. Was he building his own death mask even as he made a valiant last bid to escape the thing that pursued them?

And they were on the bridge and Katy was crying. Huge sobs that glistened and crystalised against her soft white cheeks even as they fell. "It's so cold ..." she whimpered as they pounded across the bridge. The wooden boards bucking as they went. Pulling too hard on his sister's arm and sending her sprawling to the floor. Her hands slapping with an almighty thud onto the rotting boards. Splinters strafing her hands and sending small daggers of crimson blood across her palms.

"Get up Katy! Get up!"

Ben turned to see their fate. They were half way across the bridge now. The white noise of the water below deafening them.

The figure appeared out of the fog. Huge. Foreboding. At the foot of the bridge. Leaning into the bridge, straining to move forward to get at them. As if some physical barrier – a magnetic force held it back.

"Be gone! Be gone!" Ben stood up tall over his sister and roared.

They stood. A demonic standoff. The figure beckoning with one hand, as if to tempt them back.

And then as quickly as it had appeared. It was sinking back into the pale abyss and slithering down beneath the bridge.

Ben tenderly helped his little sister to her feet and inspected her bloodied hands. "We're safe now. It can't get us here. We'll get your bag in the morning," he said bravely. Though the prospect of entering Cavalier's Field ever again – even on the brightest day of the year filled him with stony dread.

"Don't worry Bruv. I'll get a new one. From now on. We get the bus back from school, OK?" she glowered at him.

"Deal," and they hugged a hug so tight and reaffirming that he wanted to cry.

"One more thing. We never tell dad about this"

Katy nodded.

Behind them. Across the river, in the cold, dank field where potatoes and old bones rotted. Ben and Katy's father resheathed his military sword. The decorative sword last worn the day he married their mother. "Job well done," he smiled grimly to himself, knowing his kids would never take such a foolhardy shortcut across the killing field again in their life. He turned and began to take the short trudge home himself when he noticed a strange shape approaching in the darkness. He let out a small whimper and drew his sword for the final time.

A scream echoed in the fields behind them as Ben and Katy made it into the village.

"Did you hear that?" Katy asked.

"Yeah … that could have been us you know …"

"I know …"

CANNIBAL GRAN

Pauline Barnett

Our gran says she could eat us up,
But surely that's not right?
She's warm and kind and cuddly and
We can't believe she'd bite.

She says: "I won't need sugar, as
You're both already sweet
And so I'll lick and nibble you –
I'll start off with your feet."

She says: "Big toes are meaty but
The second ones are long;
The third ones all curl round a bit
And fourth ones always pong."

She says: "The fifth is scrumptious, it's
So little, soft and pink,
And so I'll finish with that one,
Then make myself a drink."

I say: "My feet are chewy, and
My heels would be the worst,"
And then I ask: "Why don't you try
My little sister first?"

I say: "She's smooth and plumpy, and
Her bum is like a peach,
So maybe you should start with her?

Cannibal Gran

I'm sure she wouldn't screech."
Gran looks at us and smacks her lips,
We're squealing for her touch –
We know she'd never eat us up:
She loves us far too much.

SECOND CHANCES

Lucy Carman

It's official. My mum's barmy.

She has this tactic, when she tells us anything we might not want to hear. She waits until we're eating or –more precisely – until everyone except her is eating, and then she strikes. Tonight is no exception.

"So, since we've got a spare room, and we could do with the money, and it'd be nice for you kids to have someone from that generation around ..."

I push my half-eaten pizza to the side of my mouth. "Mum, what are you talking about?"

"We're fostering an old lady," Mum replies. "Mrs Morley is coming to live with us."

For a moment it's silent. I hear Dad's watch ticking. My six-year-old brother Charlie stares at nothing, the way he does when he's thinking.

"What if she wants to watch boring stuff on TV all day," he asks, "can I still watch Scooby Doo?"

"How long's she staying?" I interrupt.

"Well until, you know ..." Mum looks, pleadingly, at Dad.

"Until she dies," says Dad. Then, just loud enough for us to hear, "or until we do – with a crazy old dear and two kids to look after, I'm not sure who'll go first."

By Wednesday, everything has changed.

"Hi boys," comes Mum's muffled voice as we walk through the door. The house smells of those little purple parma-violet sweets – the ones that taste of perfume. "Mrs Morley's here. She's just ..." there's a pause, "getting settled in." Just then Mrs Morley appears, ink smeared across her cheek.

"I've put up the blackout curtains upstairs," she tells us, in the same satisfied tone Dad uses when he's managed to fix a cupboard or put up a shelf. "Just showing your mum how to turn this material into shorts for you two. Make do and mend." Mrs Morley smiles encouragingly as she holds up an old lime green sheet. Before I can object, Mum steers Mrs Morley towards the kitchen.

"How about a cup of tea?"

"Ooh, lovely," replies Mrs Morley. "No milk in mine, thank you. I'll get us all a snack." A few moments later we're presented with a plate containing a slice of cold toast from breakfast, a half-eaten biscuit, a brown banana, a small collection of raisins and two frozen fish-fingers. "Dig in," says Mrs Morley, thrusting the plate at us. "Got to build up our strength. We'll need it come nightfall when the bombs start." Charlie and I exchange a look. This lady thinks we're living in the Second World War.

Later, as we're all sitting down for tea, Mum brings the house issue up again. True to form, she waits until my mouth is full of shepherd's pie.

"So Sam, I hear you've been to that house again? You know, the one you were told you were never allowed to go in?"

"What?" It's a feeble response but it's all I can think of. Mum's staring at me in that way that makes me feel she can see every thought inside my head. I decide lying my

Out of this Word

way out of this won't work. I settle for diversion. "Heard it from who?"

"It doesn't matter who, Sam. What matters is that you were in that dangerous, derelict house again."

"Well, that's it then," says Dad. "He's got to learn. He'll have to miss Ted's party."

"No!" I screech. I can't help it. "I've been looking forward to that laser quest party for weeks. I can't miss it. It'd be rude," I direct this at Mum. She cares about that sort of thing.

"He's got a point," begins Mum.

"He should have thought about that before he ..." But Dad never finishes his sentence. Suddenly music is blaring out from the radio and Mrs Morley, skirt pulled up and tucked into her knickers, is twirling towards us. She grabs Dad's hands, pulls him out of his chair and bumps bottoms with him. My dad looks so funny and awkward that we all burst out laughing. Dad frowns but then Mum starts dancing and Dad laughs too. Before we know it, we're all doing the conga around the kitchen table – the argument about the house forgotten. I glance at Mrs Morley (getting an eyeful of her long, frilly knickers) and think that maybe it won't be so bad having her around.

The next day though, disaster strikes. Ted's mum has to do a late shift and asks if Ted can come to us after school.

"Ted can't come here," I plead with Mum, "not with Mrs Morley dancing around in her knickers and going on about a war that finished seventy years ago." Mum sighs and rubs her eyes.

"Sam, please. I've been up half the night while Mrs Morley's been trying to unlock the front door with a fork. I don't have the energy to argue." Mum's voice softens. "I'll put *The Great Escape* on. That should keep her occupied for a while.

"And I'll hide the radio," Mum adds as I open my mouth to argue.

Later, after school, Ted and I walk through the door straight into Mum carrying one of Charlie's shoes.

"Dad's phoned," she says as she squeezes past. "His car's broken down and that job interview's in half an hour. I'll have to take him." She stops talking for a moment while her head disappears behind the sofa. "Got it!" She holds up Charlie's other shoe triumphantly before looking back at us, uncertainty creasing her forehead. "You two will be alright for half an hour, won't you? The biscuit tin's in the kitchen and, erm ..." Mum avoids my eyes, "Mrs Morley can keep an eye on you."

We look in unison at Mrs Morley who is hanging antibacterial wipes out to dry. Within ten seconds, I've come up with a plan:

1. *Send Ted to my room.*
2. *Put film on for Mrs Morley.*
3. *Grab biscuits.*
4. *Stay in room until Mum gets back.*
5. *Under no circumstances, let Ted and Mrs Morley meet.*

I could make this work. "We'll be fine Mum, you go," I tell her. As soon as Mum's gone, I begin step one of my plan. "Go on up," I say to Ted, guiding him towards the stairs, "I'll grab the biscuits." But it's no use – Ted is pulled to Mrs Morley like Charlie is to Scooby Doo.

"Who's she?" he asks as Mrs Morley begins fiddling with the radio that Mum's forgotten to hide. Time to go: somewhere, anywhere. I steer Ted towards the front door.

"Come on," I say, pushing him outside into the rain, "there's something I want to show you."

We both hesitate when we get there. I know we shouldn't go in, but it's the only thing I can think of. There's no way we can go home to Mrs Morley and her dancing. I crawl through the hole in the fence, past the *Danger* sign and into the old, abandoned house. Normally, I wait a few seconds for my eyes to adjust to the gloom but tonight Ted's right behind me and I can't let him think I'm hesitating. I can't see what's ahead but I need to keep on moving. The next thing I know I feel myself fall ...

My leg feels as if it's on fire. And in the darkness I see a light coming towards me. Now I'm really scared. I've heard about people seeing a light when they're dying. Thinking about it though, I don't think it's ever been accompanied by the smell of parma-violets.

"Suck on that," says a voice I know. A sweet, which is only slightly fluffy, is popped into my mouth. "Take your mind off things." In the torchlight I get a chance to really look at my rescuer. And what I see, in Mrs Morley's wrinkled face, is that her eyes haven't got old with the rest of her. They're still sparkling and bright and, for a moment, they lock with mine. "Tottenham, London, 1940," she says, as her eyes look away for a moment. "That's the last time I was in a cellar. Two boys, buried, their house on top of them: ran down there when they heard the bombs – poor beggars. It took hours to find the youngest – five years old and hidden inside a wardrobe that had fallen clean on top of him. Created the perfect hiding place." A faint smile tugs at Mrs Morley's lips at the same time as a tear rolls down her cheek. "He always loved hide and seek." Mrs Morley's head collapses into her hands. "I was their big sister. I was meant to be looking after them. Mother left me in charge. I'd only popped out for milk." Tears are streaming down her face now. "I should have been there."

I reach out.

"You're here now," I tell her. And her hand takes hold of mine.

Mrs Morley smiles as we hear the ambulance arrive. Outside Mum and Charlie are waiting. Ted's there too telling anyone who'll listen that Mrs Morley is Supergran! I reach for her as she clambers into the ambulance with me.

"I'm not leaving," she tells the ambulance man, squeezing my hand, "not this time."

THE STORY OF A KING WHO PLAYED STATUES WITH A LITTLE GIRL

Joyce Fox

In a faraway country, where rivers turn to ice and snow covers the land for six whole months of the year, there once lived an unkind King. His favourite game was Statues and he played it with someone chosen from the poor, hungry, cold people over whom he ruled. The prize was dinner with the King but no-one ever won because the King cheated. It made him so happy to see their disappointment that he rolled about on the floor, kicked his heels in the air, and laughed.

On this particular day he was in the mood to play his cruel game so he ordered Percy, a palace servant, to go out and bring back someone with whom he could play Statues.

"Make sure you find a person who looks hungry and cold," he said.

This was not hard to do as all the King's subjects looked, and were, hungry and cold. It was often snowing and not much food grew in such an icy land. Percy left the palace and looked for someone suitable. An east wind howled and sleet lashed down from a low, grey sky. The street was empty. If he went back and told the King that he couldn't find anyone, he would have to be the one to play Statues, and he *definitely* did not want to do that. He sheltered as best he could beside the palace wall, and waited.

Percy was soaking wet before something resembling a big green bird flapped past. Luckily for him, he guessed it was a little girl struggling to keep a huge, hooded cape wrapped around herself.

"Hey, you, girl. Stop!" he yelled, running after her.

"What's your name, girl?" he asked when he caught up with her.

"B B B Betty," she stuttered.

"Are you hungry?"

"Y y yes," Betty managed to answer though her teeth chattered uncontrollably. It was obvious she was cold, so Percy didn't bother to ask.

"Come with me," he ordered and pulled her through the palace gates. Once they were inside, he marched her to the King's banqueting hall.

"When I open this door you will see the King sitting on his throne behind a long table. Do not move until he beckons you, and when he holds up his hand to stop you, keep *absolutely* still. If you move at all, you will be thrown out but if you can reach the table, obeying these rules, you will be allowed to eat whatever you want from the King's table."

Percy felt sorry for Betty because he knew the King cheated when he played the game of Statues. Nobody had ever reached the table or had anything to eat. They were always thrown out just as hungry as when they came in.

He knocked on the door, 'rat a tat tat', and threw it open with a flourish. Before she had time to feel nervous, Betty was pushed into the banqueting hall. It was the longest room she had ever seen – longer than all the rooms in her house put together. At the far end, behind an enormous table, sat the King. He looked warm and comfortable on a high gold throne padded with purple velvet cushions.

"Bring in the food," the King roared.

Men appeared as if by magic. They were dressed in tall white hats and aprons that came down to their shoes. Betty's eyes were as round as marbles but she didn't even blink when they ran past her carrying trays of steaming food to the table.

They brought tureens of hot soup, platters of roast beef and bowls of fluffy, mashed potatoes. Then they ran back to the kitchen for jugs of gravy. Betty couldn't put a name to any of the wonderful aromas. She longed to inhale but resisted the temptation and didn't even allow her nose to twitch as food continued to be brought to the table.

Next, they brought warm, spiced puddings, pies filled with apples, and jugs of hot, thick custard. Finally, they scurried past her holding wobbly red and yellow jellies high above their heads. Betty couldn't wait to try every single thing.

The table was now completely smothered with food and the King, who had been watching the mounting display with almost as much fascination as Betty, now turned his attention to her. He lifted his right hand as high as his nose and slowly curled his finger in a clear signal for her to come to him.

She took three little steps before he put up his hand with his palm towards her. Betty came to an abrupt halt with one foot in the air and the King made her stand like that for a full minute before he curled his finger for a second time. Once again she took a few small steps and, once more, he lifted his palm to stop her. Betty held her breath and didn't move until she was beckoned forward by the King. Over and over, as the King curled his finger or raised his palm, she started and stopped, taking little steps forward each time and getting nearer and nearer to the table.

The Story of a King

The smell of the food was making the King exceedingly hungry and when he was hungry he did not like to be kept waiting before tucking in to his food. He could also see that Betty was excellent at playing Statues so he decided it was time to cheat. He would let her reach the table and then tell her she hadn't seen his signal to stop. She would be thrown out, and he would be able to get on with his dinner.

What happened next was unbelievable. At least when the cooks told the scullery maids, and the scullery maids told just about everyone else in the palace, none of them believed it, but this is what happened:

When Betty reached the table, she swung her head from side to side, saw the spread of food, and, before the King could say a word, she turned and ran back down the long room. As she ran, she called over her shoulder,

"Don't start your dinner 'til I get back, Your Majesty. I won't be long."

The king was dumbfounded. This should have been the time for him to roll about on the floor, kicking his heels in the air and laughing at the joke he had played on the little girl, but, instead of this, he appeared to have turned into a statue – an extremely silly looking statue – sitting with its mouth open like a fish and eyes that nearly popped out of its head. Luckily, Betty could run fast and she was back before anyone (apart from the cooks, who no one believed) saw the King looking so foolish.

This time Betty didn't wait for the king to curl his finger at her. She ran back down the room to the food-filled table and placed a little basket in front of the king. The basket was covered with a blue and white checked cloth and when the king removed it, the smell of freshly baked bread wafted up to his nostrils.

"Mmmmmm," he sniffed. "Lovely," he said. "Where? What? Why?" he stammered, looking at Betty.

"Well, Your Majesty, our soup is watery, not a bit like yours and we don't have roast meat – ever. We do have potatoes but they're not fluffy like yours and we never have puddings, pies, custard or jellies, but we do have freshly baked bread every day. I felt sorry for you because you didn't have any. That's why I ran home and fetched you this loaf. It's fresh out of the oven. We have it dry because we can't afford butter and it even tastes good like that but I expect you've got butter to spread on it and then, I imagine, it will be delicious."

Betty smiled at the King but he did not smile back. Two big tears slid down his fat cheeks. He took out an enormous red handkerchief, put it to his nose and made a noise like a badly played trumpet. From that precise moment the King became kind. It might have had something to do with blowing his nose – he did give it a blow that was strong enough to clear his head of anything nasty – but most probably it was the little girl's act of kindness that taught him a lesson.

The King shared his dinner with Betty and from that day he made sure that everyone in his kingdom had enough to eat. He also gave them warm clothing to protect them from the icy weather. He continued to play Statues but he never cheated and *always* shared his dinner – no matter who won.

HARRIET

Laura Harrhy

Her head is down and she's tripping along, hands in pockets. My eyes follow the white cable from her hip to her ears. Her eyes survey the steps she takes, step, step, toe-scuff, stumble, step, step, step.

She started at school last week, and I think she's pretty nice, but I work in a pack, and there's no way I can admit it to anyone. I think Tom probably likes her too; he's being so obvious about it though. All he's done this week is get on her nerves, saying stuff that makes him smile but makes her frown, and he shoved her to the ground in boys v girls hockey today.

I haven't seen her smile yet.

Tom turns his head towards me but doesn't take his eyes off her, "Let's follow the new girl."

He speeds up and the five of us boys follow, because we are in his orbit.

Her head lifts and turns to the left very slightly. She senses us. She turns and throws a glance behind her.

Six tall fourteen-year-olds are getting nearer. She speeds up. So do we. She runs.

Tom calls out, "Hey idiot!"

She isn't stupid, I think.

He tries again, "Oi you!"

I believe her name is Harriet.

She doesn't acknowledge him, she just keeps running. But Tom craves attention. As he chases, he throws a coin at her. A lucky shot, it hits her square on the back of the head. Without slowing her pace, Harriet's hand disappears among the flying brown wisps of her hair. A second later she disappears into the woods, just as rain fills the air like condensing steam.

Tom's trainers pound heavily on the pavement as he stops short: he hates rain. "My hair!" is all he can gasp, because he is truly unfit, and with shoulders stooped and brow wrinkled and his hands hovering protectively over the six inches of blow-dry insulating his meagre brains, he turns and slopes away towards his uncle's house. The four other boys look from him to me like expectant puppies. I shrug and they decide their loyalty lies with Tom, so off they go.

French homework aside, I haven't anything particular to do, and I'm worried about Harriet all of a sudden. Perhaps less worried, more curious. Perhaps less curious, more tired of the male diva and four groupies I hang out with. In any case, I go into the woods.

It isn't a very large patch of trees, more of a fill-in between the road and the beach, and I am soon dumped out on to sand. In the distance, further along the coast, Harriet is picking her way over the large rocks. I know the rocks well and I catch up easily, but when I call out to her she doesn't look back.

"Where are you going? It's a dead end that way."

But she continues, me a short way behind, and soon we've passed under a couple of natural arches and are standing in a sort of carved out grotto on a horseshoe ledge, mesmerised as we look down at a small, deep lagoon. Foamy water pushes and pulls against the rocks, smashing all other sounds to nothing.

She looks at me properly for the first time since I've known her, and I'm surprised to see that she's almost smiling. Almost.

Harriet

And then as the heavy winter waves crash, she leaps off the ledge.

I follow.

It's true what they say about the shock of jumping into cold water, it takes your breath away. I want to scream in shock, but for the first second I merely go rigid, my hands splayed out in claws, and then I curl up, drawing my knees tightly to my chest and trying to swim with the jagged motions of frozen arms. But a small arm around my chest drags me backwards, and the tight grip my lungs have on their little gasp of old oxygen releases, and my chest feels free again.

Opening my eyes is painful; they sting and itch, but through murkily dark air they show me a high roof made of glistening white limestone dribbled into place like candle wax. Second-hand light sneaks in through a network of slim cracks in the rock where the roof slopes down to meet the water on one side. It's all we have to see by.

A gentle insistence laps at my feet and when I sit up I establish that what my eyes are trying to see is a large expanse of black water, stretching off into the darkness in the three directions ahead and around. Harriet is crouching at the edge of the water, rinsing blood off her hands.

"Are you alright?" is my reaction, and I start forwards.

"Yes, thanks. This is your blood actually," she says through a quiet laugh, and she comes to sit a short distance from me.

The knee of my trousers is torn, and diluted blood trickles, feathery, over the wet skin. "It's nothing much," I say, since the cold is complaining louder than my knee to the receptors in my brain.

She gives me that almost-smile again; at least I think she does as I can barely see, but then the glint of faraway light in her eye disappears for a moment, re-appearing on a sliver of tooth. She's laughing, and the muffled sound echoes across the expanse of water.

"You know, your friends are idiots," she says and at first I can only shiver and nod mutely in agreement. I eventually speak.

"Yeah I'm sorry. Tom – er – I think he just wants to talk to you."

She sighs and gets to her feet. "So why did *you* follow me, Seb?"

I shrug as my teeth chatter wildly. "I didn't want to do my French homework."

Her laugh is like a thunderclap, and in the scattered rain of the laughter that follows she tells me that I'm an idiot too, but the good kind. "I've lived here all my life," she says. "But I thought I ought to try a real school for a change. It's awful actually. Although the food's alright I suppose."

"What do you mean *here*?" I ask, looking around in wonder.

Another thunderclap. "By the sea! Did you think I meant here in this cave? No, I come here to get away from people like you."

"Thanks very much, though I have to point out, since I'm here with you, that you failed miserably on that count. How do we get out of here anyway?"

She points towards the cracks of light and tells me there's an underwater entrance. All I can see is blackness. "If you're afraid, we'll wait for the tide to go out. But it'll be dark by then, and the mermaids might get you."

Harriet

I laugh at her stupid idea but in the gloom I half believe it. "We'll wait. It's dark in here anyway, and since I almost drowned on the way in, I won't tempt fate again."

As we invent sceptres and imaginary visions to bulk out a difficult game of I-spy, the weak dribble of light from outside gradually dies, and with the falling tide the water is pulled away from the banks of the underground lake to reveal a small opening in the rock. I can't see where Harriet points, but she takes my arm and points it for me. The dark has us almost blind now but I can make out subtle shades of black and their contrast with the weak glow of white from Harriet's blouse. We stand in silence.

"Are you ready?" Her whisper barely carries as far as my eardrums. I give a pointless nod.

But she doesn't move towards the black mouth of the opening. She still has hold of my wrist, and she pulls me round to face the vast, velvet dark of the water. I can't tell if my eyes are open or closed, but then something shoots past from deep within the murk. The grip on my wrist grows tighter.

Another flash, far underwater. And another. Strange things, shimmering softly as they pass, swimming as fast as my heart races.

Something surfaces, bobs for air; a swimmer, human surely, with long curls of dark hair sticking wetly to its phosphorescent shoulders. It dives downwards again, and the rest of its body follows the curve. I feel my mouth open in surprise as my eyes see soft, shining scales and a fluid, strong tail. Another being rises to the surface and pauses. It looks at us.

I have never seen such an expression: despite the dark, the being's delicately glowing face conveys happiness, sadness and welcome. I've somehow forgotten about the gap in the rocks for now.

Harriet has slackened her grip on my wrist, but I twist my hand around to grasp at her fingers and I squeeze gently. She returns the action, and without pausing for breath we step back and then one two three, we jump in.

DON'T TELL SARAH

Susan Hoffmann

The last time I saw Jimmy Jenkins he was crying. I stood on the wall, hanging on to the railings, and watched as his mother bundled him into the car and drove off. Isn't eleven too old to cry?

"That's *your* fault."

I turned round. Priya Sumati was standing staring at me. "What?" I said, jumping down and landing deliberately close to her.

"It's your fault he's going to another school," she said, and ran off. I couldn't be bothered chasing her. Instead, I wandered over towards the benches. They were all full, but two of the Year 4 kids saw me coming and sensibly opted to sit on the grass instead.

Dave Culshaw and Karl Williams came over then to ask me to join their team. (I remember Dave once saying that girls shouldn't play football. I'd made him regret that remark.)

I played in goal for a while and then got fed up and went back to the railings. Two dogs were sniffing around and having a bit of a game on the patch of waste ground opposite the school yard. One was a huge thing, black and tan, with great slobbery jowls, and the other was brown and scrawny looking. Then this puppy came out of one of the gardens along the road. It obviously wanted to play but the brown dog growled and it cowered down. It tried to go to the big slobbery one but the brown dog kept snarling and wouldn't let it past. The puppy only wanted to be friendly but the brown dog pounced on it and the poor thing yelped. It struggled free and raced away. The other two dogs trotted off together.

Mum and Dad were arguing again when I got home from school.

"It's about time you stood up for yourself," Mum was shouting. "You let everyone there walk all over you."

As usual, Dad's voice was quieter. "I don't feel I can …"

I didn't wait to hear any more. I'd told Karl and Dave and a few others to meet in the park for a game so I shouted that I'd be back by six, grabbed my bag and football, and went out.

I knew why Mum was cross. A couple of people had recently been promoted ahead of Dad even though he's been at the factory longer. Mum keeps going on about it. Dad never answers back, and that seems to make her madder than ever. He's a bit like that puppy I saw on the waste ground. Wants to be friends with everyone but turns tail and runs when things get tough.

The quickest way to the park from my house is past the school. A couple of kids were in the front garden of one of the big houses near the school. I'd seen them around but they don't go to our school so I don't know them.

"You stupid thing!" the girl yelled.

Was she talking to me? I could feel my face go red with anger. I stopped and turned back. She was waving a mangled shoe around and looked so ridiculous that I started to laugh. Then the boy bent down and scooped up a puppy. Not just any puppy – the one that was bullied by the big dog outside school. He held it out so that its nose was near the shoe.

"That's *your* fault," he said, and started shaking the poor thing. It whimpered.

"Leave it alone." The words came out of my mouth before I could stop them.

The boy looked a bit surprised.

"What did you say?" he said, walking across to the low fence and leaning over towards me.

"Leave it alone," I said again. "It's not the dog's fault if the smelly shoe was left around. Puppies always chew things. You're just a lout."

I ran off then. I'd a game to go to, hadn't I?

Near the school gates I had to stop to tie my lace and I noticed a piece of paper on the ground. I'm not much into clearing up litter or anything but the writing looked familiar so I picked it up. *4.30 at my house*, it read. *Don't tell Sarah.*

Karl and the others weren't in the park when I got there so I dumped my bag by one of the trees and sat down to wait. That puppy was going to get itself hurt if it didn't toughen up. What would happen to the puppy if it did start to answer back, though? If it growled at other dogs it was likely to get into fights and get injured, and it would probably earn itself a reputation for being nasty. Worse still, if it started to bite that girl or Lout when it was teased it might get put to sleep. It wasn't fair to bully it like that when it couldn't defend itself.

I took the scruffy note out of my pocket. *Don't tell Sarah.*

Karl and Dave wouldn't be coming to the park. Billy Green wouldn't either. Nor would Cathy or Pete or Andrea, and I could guess where they'd all gone. It was Priya Sumati's birthday. She's popular with most of the

Out of this Word

class and no doubt she'd be having a party – a big one. *Don't tell Sarah*. It was Priya's writing.

I stuffed the note and the ball into my bag and headed for home.

Lout and his sister weren't in their garden this time but the puppy was there, chewing a stick.

"Don't chew sticks," I told it. "You'll get splinters."

The puppy cringed away as if expecting to be beaten. A bit like Jimmy Jenkins. Not that I'd ever actually hit him.

The puppy dropped the stick and crawled on its belly toward the fence, wagging its spindly little tail – and I couldn't resist.

Mum was out when I got home. She works at a nursing home and sometimes does evening shifts. Dad was cooking. I tried to sneak past but he saw me and called me into the kitchen.

"You're late, Sarah."

"Sorry, Dad," I said. "I'll just put my bag upstairs then I'll come and help."

The bag whined. I coughed loudly to cover the noise but Dad wasn't fooled.

"Sarah?"

I unzipped the holdall and the puppy stuck out its head. Dad picked it up and it went all squirmy and licked his nose.

"I found it in the park," I said. "It wasn't with anyone. I think someone must have dumped it there."

"It's a her, not an it," said Dad.

"Oh. Can I keep her?"

For a moment I thought Dad would say yes. He loves animals but we've never had any because Mum says they take too much looking after.

"She's got a collar on," Dad said.

I felt a bit sick. The thin, brown collar had been hidden in the puppy's shaggy hair and I'd never thought to check.

The puppy wriggled as Dad squinted at the disc on the collar. "She's called Tessa, and there's an address and phone number here. We could phone, but it's only round the corner." He turned off the grill and the hob. "We'll take her back before tea."

A horrible panicky quivering invaded my stomach. Lout and his sister would recognise me. They'd know I'd taken her deliberately.

"Take your stuff out of your bag," said Dad. "She'll be safer if we carry her in there."

Desperately trying to think of a way out, I did as I was told. I put the football in the corner of the kitchen where we wouldn't trip over it and plonked my sweatshirt on the work surface. The note fluttered out and landed by Dad's elbow, writing side up. *Don't tell Sarah.* Maybe eleven's not too old, because I started to cry.

Dad's a good listener. When I'd stopped blubbering, I told him about stealing Tessa and about the note and about my so-called friends keeping it a secret about Priya Sumati's party. He didn't say anything, not right away. He just made me go with him to Lout's house.

That's when things finally began to go right.

Lout's parents both worked all day and they hadn't wanted a dog. Lout and his stupid sister were both sick of her chewing everything. They were only too happy to find a new home for her.

I thought Mum would object – and she did. What surprised me was the way Dad stood up to her. He didn't shout or anything, he just said the puppy was staying and that was that.

Out of this Word

Dad pinned Priya's note on to the posters board over my bed. He told me I had to leave it there until I really understood what it meant.

Right now, Tessa's asleep in her basket. I'm trying to concentrate on my homework but I keep stopping to look at her, to make sure she's still there, still mine. No one's ever going to bully her again.
One of these days I'll tell Dad about Jimmy Jenkins and ask how I can put things right.

THE APPRENTICE HOUSE

Jonathan Mayman

I was fascinated
by the stories
of those children,
some even younger than me,
who lived there, far from their families.
They worked such long hours
at that towering Mill
in the depths of the valley,
with its huge clanking water wheel
and endlessly clattering machines.

I looked into their faces
in a display of old black and white photos,
trying to imagine
what their lives were like.

Back home, checking photos on my phone,
I spot something odd
in a picture I took of the Girls' Dormitory
that I hadn't noticed at the time.
A child in a mobcap is peeping at me
from behind one of the wooden box-beds.

SONGS FROM THE ANIMAL KINGDOM

Gill McEvoy

Bear

Scratching his belly
he lumbers from his winter cave,
to stand astonished at the spring.

Cygnets

You long to plunge your hands
deep into the soft grey scruff of them,
the pale wool fluff of them

but it's wiser to respect
the distance
that the cob has set.

> *Cob – the male swan*

The Lemmings' Song

We must reach the sea by morning.
We must reach the sea by morning.
And there'll be no turning back.
And there'll be no ... huh?

Songs from the Animal Kingdom

Arctic Hare

has come down from the moon
in priestly robes of white
to pass unnoticed in the snow.

Pheasant

He stands sentry in the roadway,
his chain mail glinting in the sun
– oh, foolish bird!

Hedgehog

Fat body on tiny feet,
snuffling and grunting
in the hedge.

Lion

Golden and glorious
he sleeps all day in the sun.
While his wife gets dinner.

Lioness

Look at him, the lazy devil,
never does a thing.
Ah, but isn't he handsome!

Out of this Word

Frog

The water lilies have closed,
their heads pointing at the moon.
Gnats gather. And the frog waits.

Condor

Like a thunder cloud
he blackens the mountain tops
with his wide, dark wings.

Flamingos

You might think it very hard that we
stand so long on just one leg
with an appearance of pink laundry
held up by wooden peg!

Slug

When it comes to courtship
a slug's no fool –
he covers his mate with slimy drool!

Yet nobody loves a slug –
we tread on the things in our garden clogs
or drown them all in beery bogs.

Songs from the Animal Kingdom

Snakes

Keep a sharp eye. Mind your step. Do not wake
the curled-up-basking-in-the-sun snake,
the snake-in-the-sneaky-grass snake,
the wrapped-round-the-branches-of-a-tree snake.

Pond-skater

How clever, skating
on the pond
when there is no ice.

WITCH WAY

Irene Moor

A lone stone cottage on a high and windy moor
A lighted parlour window, a lantern at the door.
A row of gnarled old oak trees lined a broken brick laid path
And watching by an iron gate, a large black, green eyed cat.
The heavy door was opened and an owl flew from the thatch
As a bent old crone approached the house and rattled at the latch.
Inside, a wide log fire burned crackling low and bright
And round the hearth three witches sat, this was their special night.
One was roasting chestnuts for this meeting once a year,
All of them excited now, as Christmas was so near.
And so they sat till midnight, working, weaving yarns and telling
Tales of ancient magic lore and practising their spelling.
When the spells were quite complete they were sealed up into jars
Addressed to Father Christmas and stamped with silver stars.

In a while an imp appeared; he had a great red sack.
The witches helped him fill it up and heave it on his back.
He thanked them very much indeed and then he said goodbye,
He hoped he'd see them here next year but now he had to fly
Back to Father Christmas to help him pack the sleigh
With all the toys that girls and boys like most on Christmas Day.
Long after the imp had left them and just before first light,
All the witches sighed and said they'd had a lovely night.

Witch Way

But now the silver frost was peeping down the tree lined row,
The dawn would soon be creeping and it was time to go
So silently they stole away, across the windy moors
On swiftly flying broomsticks back to their own front doors.

So if you see a cottage standing all alone,
With mullioned parlour windows and strong stout walls of stone,
Remember who may live there, as you'd never quite believe
The happy spells the witches weave for us to share on Christmas Eve!

CAT BY THE GARDEN POOL

Don Nixon

He slinks out from the shadow of the shed,
peers down, tail twitching, readying every claw.
The water mirrors and reflects his head.
He slowly preens and then extends a paw.

About to strike, he halts. His eyes meet mine
and seek approval. He will kill for me.
Fish on my pillow. This his usual sign,
Like mice on mats or birds caught in the tree.

He strikes a pose, just waiting for my nod
to compliment his lithe and sinuous grace.
Worship as for some Nile ancestral god
he thinks his due. Slit pupils read my face.

I stamp and shout. He stares then darts away.
Not too far. He crouches, then looks up high
To where the birds perch round the feeding tray.
Forgets the pool. He's other fish to fry.

FLYPIE AND DOODLEBUG

Lynn Shelley

It was Doodlebug's fault. There we were, sitting on the wall, swinging our legs and bemoaning the fact we only had twenty pence between us when he said,

"I've got an idea." I groaned because Doodlebug's ideas always get us in to trouble. "Mrs Broadhead has a plum tree in her garden. And she's away."

"So?" I said.

"So, my mum said that plums make the most amazing jam," said Doodlebug.

"And?"

"So, Flypie, you wally ..." Doodlebug had a grin plastered all over his face. "... All we've got to do is to sneak into Mrs Broadhead's garden, pick a whole load of plums and sell them in Macclesfield market to people who like making jam. We'll make a fortune."

"That's stealing," I said. "People get arrested for taking things that aren't theirs."

"But they don't get arrested for clearing up other people's gardens," said Doodlebug. "We'll be doing her a favour. She's away for a whole month, visiting her sister in Australia. If we don't pick the plums off her tree, they'll fall to the ground and rot. They'll make a huge mess on her lawn and when she comes back she'll have to pay gardeners to clear it up. We'll be saving her money."

"No," I said. "Definitely not," I said. "I'm not going into her garden and I'm not taking her plums."

Two nights later, Doodlebug was scrambling over the wall into Mrs Broadhead's garden and I was standing below keeping watch.

"Throw the bucket after me," he ordered.

I waited 'til he dropped down into the garden and tossed the bucket over the wall. There was a thud and a yelp.

"Idiot!"

The moon was painting black shadows on the lawn. It was nearly midnight and everyone else was in bed, which is where we should have been. But I was soon up in the tree throwing plums down to Doodlebug and he was catching them in the bucket. Then we heard a crash. Someone was smashing a window. Doodlebug dropped to the ground and I flung myself flat, clinging to the branch, hoping that no-one could see me. It was quiet. Dead quiet. Until I heard heavy breathing and someone moaning as if he'd hurt himself. And the noise was coming from the side of Mrs Broadhead's house.

I waited for my heart to stop pounding at my ribs and then slowly slithered down the trunk.

"Someone's trying to get into Mrs Broadhead's house," I whispered. "We've got to stop him."

"You're mad," croaked Doodlebug. "He could have a crowbar. Or a gun. Or a knife."

Usually it's Doodlebug who's the mad one. That's why his granddad started calling him 'Doodlebug'. A doodlebug was a sort of bomb they used to flatten cities in the last war. And he's a sort of disaster – like they were. But this time it was me who was the mad one, because I liked Mrs Broadhead and I didn't want her to be burgled.

"I'm not letting some screwball pinch stuff from Mrs Broadhead," I said. "Are you going to help me or not?"

Flypie and Doodlebug

We wriggled along underneath the hedge until we got to the side of the house. The window to her dining room had been smashed in, and the rough edges of the glass had been taken out.

"Go on, then." Doodlebug elbowed me in the ribs. "Take a look."

I snaked across the grass and stuck my head over the sill. The moonlight bounced cold light over the glass pieces on the carpet, but there was no sign of the intruder. Doodlebug pushed past me.

"Let's go inside," he whispered.

We slid over the window sill, hurtled across the room to the table and dived under it. After a couple of minutes the door opened and a pair of legs came towards us. The sound of heavy breathing scared me half to death. It didn't sound like a man. It sounded like a gorilla. But a gorilla doesn't wear trainers.

"No-one's here," the man shouted.

There was a short silence, then the legs strode over to the window. "No-one's outside either," he called. "I'm coming back up."

We listened as he climbed the stairs.

"There's two of them," said Doodlebug.

"Let's call the police." I pulled out my mobile. Doodlebug snatched it away.

"And say what?" he hissed. "We were pinching plums from Mrs Broadhead's tree and now we're in her house with a couple of burglars? They'll throw us into prison, too."

"I thought you said we were helping her," I said. "You told me we'd be saving her money."

Doodlebug shook his head. "What a moron," he said. "You knew we were doing something wrong when we climbed over her wall. If we'd just been helping her, we'd have gone through the gate and picked her plums in the day time, wouldn't we?"

Suddenly I felt sick. I'm called 'Flypie' because once I found a huge, hairy legged fly in a school apple pie and threw up all over the hall floor. Now I feel sick whenever something worries me.

"Don't you dare throw up here," ordered Doodlebug, glaring at me. "And stop worrying. I've got another plan."

I almost groaned, but I was scared that if I did, I *would* be sick.

"We're not going to call the police," said Doodlebug. And I could tell that he was grinning by the sound of his voice. "Because we're going to *be* the police."

Then he told me his plan, and suddenly, I was grinning too.

He crawled from underneath the table and disappeared out through the window. Five minutes later he was back.

"Done it!" he said. "Now let's have some fun."

There's something I haven't told you about me and Doodlebug. When we grow up, we're going to go on *Britain's Got Talent*. We're going to be a double act – you know, when two people go on stage and tell jokes and do sketches and make people laugh. We want to be comedians like Ant and Dec or Morecambe and Wise. We've been practising imitating people's voices so we can use them in our sketches. And because P.C. Jones, our local policeman comes from Wales and has got a really strong accent, Doodlebug's been practising speaking like him. And I've been practising speaking like Mrs Pendleton-Smythe – as if I've got a pebble in my mouth – so we can use these voices on the show.

Flypie and Doodlebug

We crept into the hall and hid behind the long curtains in front of the windows. Above us we could hear the voices of the men upstairs, and rustling and soft banging as they searched for Mrs Broadhead's jewellery.

Then Doodlebug puffed out his chest and opened the curtains a bit. He stuck his head out and started shouting. And if I didn't know it was him, I would have sworn it was P.C. Jones.

"So, Mrs Pendleton-Smythe," he said, his voice rolling loud like thunder on the mountains. "You think someone's been trying to burgle Mrs Broadhead's house, do you?"

Suddenly the noise upstairs stopped.

Then I stuck my head out. "Oh, P.C. Jones," I warbled, my voice sounding like a woman with two pebbles in her mouth and a nasty attack of the shrieks. "I'm sure I saw torchlight shining through the curtains upstairs. Shall we take a look?"

The whole house stopped breathing, but Doodlebug and I were nearly cracking up.

"You come outside with me," barked 'P.C. Jones'. "Where you'll be safe. I'll radio for help."

Doodlebug made a creaking sound as if the front door was opening and closing, and for a whole minute everything was so quiet you could have heard a spider snore.

Then two sets of footsteps crashed down the stairs. The men were trying to run down quietly, but they were in such a rush to escape they were tumbling over each other. We heard them race into the dining room and scramble over the windowsill and out into the night.

"Now you can call the police," said Doodlebug, handing me my mobile phone, and he was snorting with laughter. "Use David Beckham's voice this time."

Out of this Word

And when I'd finished we tore out of the house, threw ourselves over the wall and collapsed in a heap on the pavement. We were laughing so hard we nearly died. In the distance we heard the wail of a police siren.

It was in all the papers. How two burglars were apprehended by police after an anonymous tip-off that they were robbing a house. Someone had let down the tyres of their van and the police had caught them as they ran down the road.

No-one's discovered that Doodlebug and I are heroes and we can't tell anyone. But we reckon we must be ready to 'Showcase our talents to the world' as Ant and Dec would say. So I've sent off the forms and we're entering *Britain's Got Talent*. Watch out for the double act: Flypie and Doodlebug.

UPADOWNALONG

Martin Staton

Walk upside down along backwards lane,
Start at the bottom where there's nothing to gain.
Hear the cat whistle, and see the dog sing
As it rains from the ground and dries everything.

The sun shines at night, and the moon lights the day
And stars hang from trees to light up our way.
Where birds live in houses and dragons in trees
And mice eat potatoes and chickens like cheese.

Close your eyes tight, and look up at the sky
Where the clouds dance with rainbows, but never pass by.
They dance through the air, and they dance on the ground.
They dance to a sweetness and silence of sound.

Walk upside down along backwards lane,
If you don't do it right now you may never again.
For this place where nothing appears as it seems
Can only be found in the magic of dreams.